JESSE BOOT

OF NOTTINGHAM

Founder of The Boots Company

**The close association between
The Boots Company and the
City of Nottingham began over a
century ago when Jesse Boot
opened his first shop in Goose Gate.**

Christopher Weir

Acknowledgements

The Boots Company is grateful to the many people who have contributed to Jesse Boot of Nottingham. *In the preparation of this publication Professor Stanley Chapman's book,* Jesse Boot of Boots The Chemists, *has been an invaluable reference source. Other organisations whose help we would wish to acknowledge are:*

Nottinghamshire Archives, Nottinghamshire County Council Leisure Services
Local Studies, Nottinghamshire County Council Leisure Services
Museum of Costume and Textiles, Nottingham City Council
Brewhouse Yard Museum, Nottingham City Council
Elvaston Castle Estate Museum
The University of Nottingham Department of Manuscripts and Special Collections
The design of the birth certificate is Crown copyright and is reproduced with the permission
of the Controller of HMSO

Designed: Design Services, The Boots Company PLC; Cunningham Design
Photography and reproduction: A V Communication, The Boots Company PLC; Declan Joyce;
JMS Photography; Mallard Imaging
Printed: Hill & Tyler Ltd, Nottingham

Published by The Boots Company PLC, Nottingham, NG2 3AA
ISBN 1 873116 01 2

CONTENTS

Sir Jesse Boot, Lord
Trent of Nottingham,
1850 -1931.

**Painting by
N Denholm Davies**

PREFACE

The Boots Company is one of the UK's largest companies with an annual turnover of billions of pounds and many thousands of staff worldwide. In addition to Boots The Chemists, its interests include different types of retailing, property management, pharmaceuticals and the manufacture and marketing of a wide range of consumer products.

The Company's headquarters and principal manufacturing site have always been in Nottingham where roots were firmly established more than 100 years ago. This booklet tells the remarkable story of Jesse Boot and explores both his personal life and his achievements in creating one of the country's most successful businesses.

Jesse Boot started with a single shop in one of Nottingham's poorest areas surrounded by poverty and disease. By following the principles of buying in bulk and selling for cash, Jesse was able to provide affordable medicines for the poor. He made many of his own products on the premises of his Goose Gate store on the edge of the Lace Market. Jesse was a man of iron determination and boundless energy, though in later life he faced a painful struggle against the crippling effects of rheumatoid arthritis. Undoubtedly he drew great strength from deep religious convictions and from his wife, Florence.

No matter how large his retail empire became, Jesse was always conscious that his company's roots were firmly planted in Nottingham, the town in which he had grown up. Towards the end of his life he donated substantial funds to local charities, provided land for new public parks and a large country estate at Highfields for the building of new premises for the University College of Nottingham, devoting endless hours in his retirement to its planning and development.

Today the Company still plays its part in providing a better quality of life by supporting a whole range of community projects and educational initiatives and donating more than £1 million every year to charitable organisations. It takes pride in its association with the City of Nottingham and works closely with local authorities, the universities and many other Nottingham based organisations. In all its activities, commercial and social, The Boots Company continues to draw inspiration from its founder, Jesse Boot.

EARLY
DAYS

1850. BIRTHS in the *District* of *Byron* in the Count *Town* of *Nottingham*								
No.	When Born.	Name, if any.	Sex.	Name and Surname of Father.	Name and Maiden Surname of Mother.	Rank or Profession of Father.	Signature, Description, and Residence of Informant.	When Registered.	Signature of Registrar.	Baptismal Name, if added after Registration of Birth.
310	Second June 1850 Woolpack Lane Nottingham	Jesse	Boy	John Boot	Mary Boot formerly Wills	Herbalist	Mary Boot mother Woolpack Lane Nottingham	Eleventh July 1850	Parr Registrar	

Jesse Boot was born in Nottingham on 2 June 1850. His father, John Boot, is described in the birth entry as a 'Herbalist'.

JESSE BOOT'S ORIGINS could not have been more ordinary or down to earth. For several generations the Boot family had worked the land as agricultural labourers in south Nottinghamshire, their lives revolving around the ever changing needs of the farming year. Jesse's father, John Boot, had been born at Radcliffe-on-Trent in 1815, where from an early age he worked at a ceaseless round of labouring jobs for local farmers. John grew up to be a sociable young man who took a full part in village life; he attended the local Methodist chapel, taught at Sunday school classes and also enjoyed music and dancing. In 1838 he married Elizabeth Mills from the neighbouring parish of Holme Pierrepont, and a few years later a daughter was born.

But though married life had started promisingly enough, the harsh nature of daily life was soon to take its toll on the young family. Agricultural labourers earned only meagre wages and their living conditions were notoriously poor. Inevitably many labouring families lived under the constant threat of illness and disease. Sadly, John Boot's own family was not to escape these brutal conditions. A few

years after his marriage to Elizabeth the couple's baby daughter died after an attack of croup, and tragedy struck a second time, in 1848, when Elizabeth died from tuberculosis. At around this time John turned increasingly to religion. Already involved in local Methodism, he began to take an interest in Methodist activities in Nottingham where Wesleyan chapels at Broad Gate and in Halifax Place, near Goose Gate, were attracting large congregations. On occasion John would walk more than four miles into Nottingham to attend services and special chapel events.

It may have been through his Methodist activities that John met and later married Mary Wills, the daughter of Benjamin Wills, a bookkeeper in a Nottingham lace firm. Jesse, their first child, was born on the 2 June 1850 and was baptised at Broad Gate Chapel. The 1851 census returns record that the family was living at 71 Woolpack Lane, a narrow thoroughfare that ran in an east to west direction down through Hockley, a district of overcrowded streets, courts and alleys that stood on the eastern side of the town.

This view of Nottingham from the south, in 1846, portrays an almost idyllic rural scene. However Nottingham's growing industrial character is revealed in a skyline of factory chimneys and warehouses.

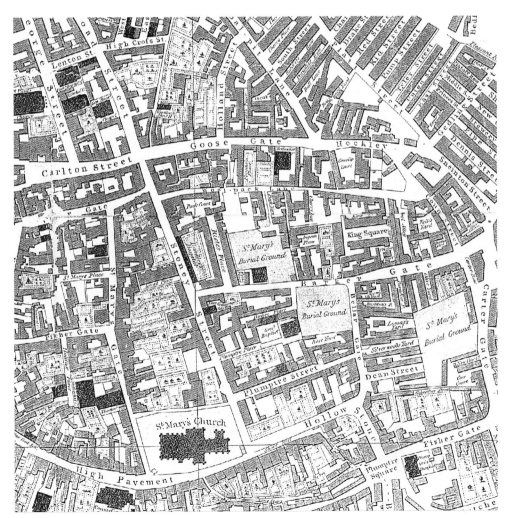

A map of Nottingham in the mid-19th century. Jesse Boot was born in Woolpack Lane, Hockley, the poor 'east end' of the town. Jesse's father opened a small herbal shop on Goose Gate, which ran parallel to Woolpack Lane, at the edge of the Lace Market.

The Thomas Adams, Page & Company warehouse, on Stoney Street, was one of the grandest lace buildings in Nottingham. The company exported lace all over the world and employed over a thousand workers.

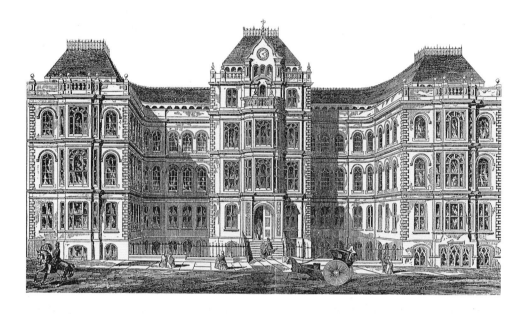

Lace workers in Knotted Alley in the 1890s.

Nottingham lace

Hockley developed in the shadow of Nottingham's emerging industrial skyline, its inhabitants drawn in from surrounding hamlets and villages to work in the growing number of factories, warehouses and workshops that powered Nottingham's expansion into an industrialised town. Much of the town's industrial strength was based on the textile industry, and above all on the production of lace, for which Nottingham gained a world-wide reputation.

By the mid-nineteenth century more than 100 lace factories and warehouses had opened in Nottingham, employing a small army of workers. And while lace factories appeared all over Nottingham and in its nearby suburbs, the sales departments, accounts offices and warehousing grew up in the heart of Nottingham itself, in what became known as the Lace Market. Here, behind St. Mary's Church, an area of old houses and small gardens was rapidly transformed into a maze of towering industrial buildings and narrow streets that formed the commercial hub of the lace trade. Leading lace firms, including Jacoby, Birkin & Co and Thomas Adams spared no expense in constructing large warehouses that were among the finest commercial buildings of their day. Thomas Birkin's Broadway premises and the Thomas Adams & Page warehouse on Stoney Street were monuments to both the importance and success of lace, not only in Nottingham but also throughout the world. Living on Woolpack Lane, on the very edge of the

Lace Market, John and Mary must have seen those great buildings take shape almost day by day and watched the daily tide of workers flowing in and out of the local streets. In future years these same people were to provide valuable trade for the first Boots shop.

But Nottingham's growth had been almost too rapid; little thought had been given to the housing or living conditions of its poorer families. The town had no fewer than 8,000 back-to-back houses, built of the cheapest materials and lacking any form of modern sanitation. In some industrial districts, like Hockley, life was a struggle for survival. If a single member of a family fell victim to an injury at work or a serious illness, it could reduce the whole family to poverty in only a few weeks.

In areas like Hockley, local chapels became important centres of religious and social life. Driven by his own Methodist impulses and a passion to help his own community, John Boot became even more involved in chapel affairs and especially in local schemes to improve the lot of his neighbours. John's religious fervour was probably inherited from Sarah, his mother, who had 'died in the triumph of faith' when he was only 17. Sarah had taken an active part in village affairs, running a local school and administering herbs and potions to the sick. Her use of herbs for healing purposes was to prove an important influence on both John, and, in turn, Jesse Boot.

'I believe that nowhere else shall we find so large a mass of inhabitants crowded into courts, alleys and lanes, as in Nottingham and those, too, of the worst possible construction. Here they are clustered upon each other; court within court, yard within yard, and lane within lane, in a manner to defy construction. The courts are almost, without exception, approached through a low-arched tunnel of some 30 or 36 inches wide, about eight feet high, and from 20 to 30 feet long, so as to place ventilation or direct solar exposure out of possibility on the space described. The courts are noisome, narrow, unprovided with adequate means for the removal of refuse, ill-ventilated, and wretched in the extreme, with a gutter or surface drain, running down the centre; they have no back yards, and the privies are common to the whole court; altogether they present scenes of a deplorable character.'

Extract from the
Report of the
Health of Towns
Commission, 1845.

Title page of John Wesley's *Primitive Physic,* first published in 1747. It was one of the most popular 'herbals' of the 18th and 19th centuries.

Extracts from Wesley's *Primitive Physic.*

In traditional folk medicine the use of herbs had been widespread for hundreds of years. Herbal remedies offered a natural approach to healing and were much favoured by the labouring poor who could not afford the services of a physician. All kinds of medicinal herbs were gathered locally from the countryside. Agrimony or 'stickwort' was collected to soothe skin rashes and was prepared as an infusion to ease coughs. Wild marjoram was used to alleviate stomach upsets and the leaves of plantain were crushed and applied as a poultice to stop bleeding.

The use of herbs for medicinal purposes had been popularised by the publication of herbals, from Elizabethan times onwards. These contained descriptions of herbs along with accounts of their medicinal and culinary properties. One of the most popular was John Wesley's *Primitive Physic,* which included remedies that Wesley, the pioneer Methodist leader, had gathered whilst preaching in villages and towns all over the country. It was first printed in 1747 but was reprinted throughout the 18th and 19th centuries. To an ardent Methodist like John Boot, the life and work of Wesley held great fascination and he would certainly have been familiar with Wesley's herbal. In the 1840s a further boost to herbalism came in the form of 'medical botany', a movement that had its origins in America, where Samuel Thomson, a farmhand turned herbalist, acquired a national reputation based on a unique blend of herbs and healing. In time his ideas reached England, finding particular success in Northern manufacturing towns, including

Nottingham. Indeed, John Boot is known to have attended a lecture in Nottingham by John Skelton, a leading campaigner for medical botany in England. John Boot immediately recognised that with the working knowledge of herbs handed down from his mother he could himself use medical botany, in combination with his religious faith, to offer physical as well as spiritual comfort to the needy. In addition he could provide himself and his family with a reasonable living.

With the assistance of his father-in-law, John Boot opened the British and American Botanic Establishment at 6 Goose Gate, a busy street which ran only a few yards to the north of Woolpack Lane, and which took an almost parallel course through Hockley. By staying in the same neighbourhood John and Mary were able to draw on strong local support, especially from the Methodist community and their remedies were in constant demand from Hockley's residents who lived under the constant threat of disease and illness. Little can John and Mary have imagined that, as they struggled to establish their tiny shop, they were laying the foundations for one of the largest retail networks in Britain.

Though they purchased some stock from suppliers, John and Mary prepared many herbal remedies themselves, as well as serving in the shop and keeping accounts. It was a difficult time for the whole family, yet, even though just running the shop alone was hard enough, John Boot devoted endless hours to the promotion of medical botany. He undertook exhausting lecture tours to publicise medical botany, established a network of local medical botany agents and even organised a Medical Botany Festival in Nottingham. However, John's health, already weakened by his days as an agricultural labourer, began to deteriorate at an alarming rate and after a succession of illnesses he died in 1860, at the age of 45 leaving Mary, Jesse, aged 10, and his sister Jane, who was only a year old.

An 1854 advertisement for John Boot's Botanic Establishment, Goose Gate.

Marjoram

With the help of friends, neighbours and her Methodist connections, Mary somehow managed to keep the Goose Gate shop going. Jesse helped wherever he could, often accompanying his mother on long trips into the countryside to gather herbs from the hedgerows, ditches and fields around Nottingham. Together they sometimes trudged for miles in search of suitable plants, Jesse often going barefoot rather than let wet grass ruin his leather boots, as they had to be carefully preserved for shop days and Sunday best.

For two years Jesse attended the Agnes Mellers Free Grammar School on Stoney Street, which later became known as Nottingham High School. The school later moved to a new site between the Arboretum and Forest. Walking each day from Goose Gate to school Jesse would have walked along Stoney Street, on the way passing grand lace warehouses that reflected the ambition and prosperity of Victorian Nottingham's powerful lace barons. Perhaps the young Jesse Boot once stared up at the great Adams & Page building, not far from the Grammar School, and dreamed that one day he too would found an industrial empire, employ thousands of people and create buildings that would carry his own family name.

Victorian school room

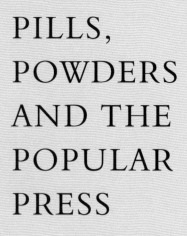

PILLS,
POWDERS
AND THE
POPULAR
PRESS

The Market Place, Nottingham.
On market days, hundreds of shoppers crowded into Nottingham to buy everything from vegetables to pots and pans. Overlooking the colourful rows of stalls is the Exchange (on the back right of the photograph), where the Council held its meetings.

WHEN JESSE LEFT HIS schooldays behind he embarked on a life of long hours, dedication and sheer hard work. For Jesse, his mother and sister Jane, the task of keeping the family business going became a matter of survival. Jesse, who was only 13, had to help with all the shop's routine tasks. The counter needed constant attention, herbal preparations were concocted on a cast-iron range in the parlour at the back of the shop, the takings had to be reckoned up every evening and the shelves kept fully stocked and in neat order. Only on Sundays would the shop's routine be broken for visits to chapel services and family outings.

Beyond the world of shop and chapel there was little time for anything else, other than the occasional visit to the Market Place where street musicians and entertainers mingled with stallholders and shoppers, and where, every autumn, Nottingham held its famous Goose Fair. For a few days each year the whole town came alive with the sights, sounds and smells of one of the largest and oldest fairs in England. By Victorian times the fair had developed into a spectacle of diversion and entertainment. As Jesse passed through the fair's tangle of people and stalls he would have seen jugglers, acrobats, dancers, travelling musicians, dwarves, giants, and he may even have joined the crowds at Wombwell's Menagerie, staring in wonder at its 'unrivalled collection of wild beasts'. However, such diversions would have been few and far between for young Jesse Boot. The shop had to come first.

As Jesse learned more and more about the shop's workings he began to take an

The Great SIGHT of the FAIR.

BOSTOCK & WOMBWELL'S
NO. I GRAND STAR

Menagerie,

AND

Circus of Varieties,

Far Larger and more Valuable than
all other travelling Collections
combined.

*In addition to the Monstre Attractions of this
Unrivalled Establishment.*

FREDERICK CARDONO

The Monarch of all Lion Kings.
Will Enter the Den at every Performance, with the

UNTAMEABLE LION.

WALLACE,

The most Thrilling Sight ever witnessed, and a Challenge
to all so-called

LION HUNTERS

To Enter the Cage with this
The most Ferocious Animal ever seen in Captivity.
All should witness this Great Performance.

THE GREAT SIGHT OF THE FAIR.

ALFRED WARREN-BAKER, " Chronicle " Office, Aston Cross.

In Victorian times Nottingham's Goose Fair was held in the Market Place. Among its attractions was Bostock & Wombwell's Menagerie, which included 'Wallace, the Untameable Lion'.

The *Herbal Almanack* of 1876 contained information on a whole range of herbal preparations. It also included an advertisement for 'Boot's Herbal Medicine Stores'.

ESTABLISHED 1849.

COMPOSITION POWDER.

The above compound is the best known Remedy for Colds, Influenza, Bowel Complaints ; and as a harmless natural stimulant it stands unrivalled.

TO BE HAD OF

M. & J. BOOT, MEDICAL BOTANISTS,
38, GOOSE GATE, NOTTINGHAM,

All the Preparations used in the Botanic Practice supplied Wholesale and Retail.

increasing share in its management. His mother was a shrewd businesswoman and she taught Jesse everything she knew about running a shop. Jesse proved a quick learner. He had a good head for figures and was an excellent judge of which stock would sell and which would lie gathering dust on the shelves. On the 2 June 1871, when Jesse reached the age of 21, his hard work was rewarded with a partnership in the business, which then began to trade under the name of Mary and Jesse Boot, Herbalists.

Even at this early stage Jesse's talent for business was evident. To gain an edge on his competitors he began to place advertisements in local trade directories and herbal almanacks. One of his methods was to use testimonial adverts based on letters of thanks from grateful customers.

One 1876 almanack included a letter from a Mr James Bacon, a Primitive Methodist preacher living on Bridlesmith Gate, in Nottingham, who proclaimed: 'I have great pleasure in bearing testimony to the medical skill of Boot's Herbal Medicine Stores, they having at various occasions prescribed for me and my family with the most satisfying results and at an extremely moderate charge'. He also used a letter that had been sent to his father by a James Searson of New Brinsley in 1852. He had been suffering from 'a violent cough' and 'hard gushing from the nose' but following treatment under 'the Botanic System' he had been able to follow his 'employment as usual' and had enjoyed 'good health ever since'. At the end of the advert Jesse had added that 'Mr Searson is now, October 1875 (a period of twenty three years), alive and well and will be glad to answer any inquiries'.

This photograph, of Parr's Yard, was taken shortly before its demolition in 1931. These sunless and enclosed courts, built in the 19th century, were breeding grounds for diseases like typhoid, scarlet fever and cholera.

Carr's Oil Blacking was one of many household products sold by Jesse and Mary, in addition to their herbs and medicines.

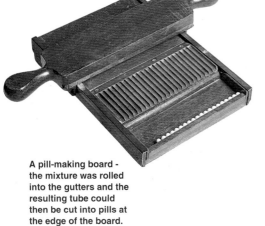

A pill-making board - the mixture was rolled into the gutters and the resulting tube could then be cut into pills at the edge of the board.

These silver coated pills were sold by some chemists to the fashionable rich, who would pay more if their pills had a shiny appearance. Jesse objected to such ploys, preferring to sell plain pills, in simple packaging, at the lowest possible cost.

Right from the start of his business career Jesse revealed an iron determination to cut prices to a bare minimum. An advertisement that ran throughout the 1870s for M & J Boot The Household Stores announced boldly that they were the store who sold 'all things cheaply, not one or two as other traders do'. Jesse's determination to cut prices was rooted in his Nottingham background. Living and working in Hockley, one of the poorest districts in the town, he was painfully aware how few families could afford the expensive medicines being sold by many local chemists, though they were the very people who needed most help. They lived crammed together in courts, yards and alleys which were breeding grounds for typhoid, cholera, scarlet fever and whooping cough. Only if the price of herbs and medicines was reduced would these people, many of them Jesse's own neighbours, be able to afford the help they so desperately needed in the daily struggle against dirt and disease.

Many of Jesse's rivals catered solely for the 'carriage trade'. They relied on fixed prices, artificially high in order to keep themselves in pocket and to restrict competition. They sold their expensive 'cures', salves and tonics to the fashionable rich who travelled by carriage from their spacious villas at the edge of Nottingham into the town centre to pick up their elegantly wrapped packages, often paying by credit rather than cash. To further encourage the carriage trade, some chemists even gave their pills a shiny silver coat, a ploy that made them look more attractive while at the same time helping to justify their high price. Jesse, on the other hand, had no such pretensions; he sold his medicines at the lowest possible prices, buying his stock in bulk to keep his own costs low. There was no fancy wrapping, just plain brown paper and an honest to goodness price that anyone could afford. As Jesse couldn't afford to give credit he asked his customers to pay cash, and, in turn, he always paid his suppliers in cash. It was a no-nonsense language that everyone understood, and in later years Jesse used his reputation for dealing in cash in the company title Boots Cash Chemists.

Under Jesse's influence the shop began to sell an ever wider range of stock including all kinds of patent medicines that were in increasing demand from customers. One advert claimed that M & J Boot carried 'Over 2,000 different articles'. Jesse began to stock more and more proprietary medicines, though always at cheaper prices than his competitors. Reflecting on this period of his life, many years later, Jesse wrote:

'I had an idea that the herbalist and chemist at that time was very much out of date... I thought the public would welcome new chemists shops in which a greater and better variety of pharmaceutical articles could be obtained at cheaper prices'.

By 1877 Jesse had built up a range of stock that rivalled any chemist in Nottingham. There was no holding him back now. In the same year Jesse took over control of the shop from his mother and though he continued to trade under the name M & J Boot for several years, the modern Boots company had been founded, and Jesse had

taken an important step forward on the road to fame and fortune. Jesse now prepared to launch M & J Boot into the forefront of Nottingham's business world. He wanted to let the whole town know about his large range of stock and low prices. So, in February 1877, he began a major advertising campaign in the 'popular press' that few potential customers, or competitors, could ignore. The campaign featured an advert in the name of M & J Boot, in which a formidable list of no fewer than 128 'patent medicines' and 'toilet requisites' demanded the reader's attention. There were pills, powders, 'purifiers', elixirs, syrups, mixtures, ointments and 'miraculous' salves. There was Allen's Hair Restorer, Clarke's Skin Lotion, Woodhouse's Rheumatic Elixir and Fennings Cooling Powder. There were Boots Patent Lobelia Pills, Bronchial Lozenges, Aromatic Composition Powders and the intriguingly named Boots No Name Ointment for 'scurvy, bad legs and blotches in the face'. There was tar soap, Juniper soap, polish, Eau de Cologne and marking ink; and there were lentils at 1s a lb. or 7lbs for 5s. In fact there was virtually everything a customer could possibly want and at a cheaper price than anyone else could offer. No expense was spared; the advert continued to appear every week, until the end of August, by which time Jesse had become the largest dealer in patent medicines in Nottingham. His campaign slogans of 'Reduced Prices' and 'Health For A Shilling' were on everyone's lips, the shop's takings had risen from £20 a week up to more than £100, and customers were queuing up at the counter.

In February 1877 Jesse launched a major advertising campaign in the *Nottingham and Midland Counties Daily Express*. It was an instant success, and by the end of the year he was one of the busiest shopkeepers in Nottingham.

Reconstruction of Jesse Boot's first shop at the bottom (east end) of Goose Gate.

In under a year Jesse had become one of the busiest shopkeepers in Nottingham. He was rushed off his feet, serving customers, ordering stock and checking accounts. If he did ever have time to glance out of his little shop window or take a stroll into the countryside, he would certainly have noticed that his home town was changing rapidly. An ever advancing tide of streets, houses and factories was spreading over the fields where once he and his mother had collected herbs.

A view down Goose Gate, where Jesse first made his name in the business world.

Nottingham was growing fast. Its population had grown from 53,000 in 1841 to around 90,000 in the 1870s. Everything was busier and noisier. On market days its narrow streets jostled with carts, wagons, carriages and horse trams; the stalls in the Market Place sold everything from poultry and cheese to pots and pans and every street corner resounded to the cries of hawkers and peddlars. While there was prosperity there was also overcrowding and poverty, and to cope with some of these problems the Town Council began a series of improvements - new schools were built, slums cleared, streets widened, and a number of public parks were opened, including the Arboretum and the Forest. And in 1877 a Borough Extension Act enabled Nottingham to extend its official boundaries to take in the surrounding parishes of Lenton, Radford, Bulwell, Basford, Carrington, Sherwood, Sneinton and part of Wilford. From its origins as a local market town, Nottingham was changing rapidly into a large regional city.

Jesse worked day and night to build on the success of his 1877 advertising campaign but above all he needed more space. Then, in 1881, a property fell vacant further up the street, at Nos 16-20 Goose Gate, nearer the town centre. This was the opportunity he had been waiting for. After taking on a 99-year lease on the site he engaged Richard Charles Sutton, a well-known local architect, to design a completely new shop. To help finance the reconstruction he drew on the support of several local business contacts, among them Henry Jalland, a prosperous wine merchant who ran a prestigious shop, also on Goose Gate, and on which Jesse may well have modelled his new store. Jesse made the most of every inch available. On the ground floor there was the retail shop, wholesale shop, 'stores' and Jesse's private office. On the first floor there were four stockrooms; and on the second floor there were two bedrooms, a sitting room and a kitchen. At the back of the premises three cottages, purchased by Jesse in 1880, were adapted to accommodate extra stock. In addition the entire length of the shop, up to 2 storeys in height was rebuilt using large sheets of glass, divided by elegant iron columns, to create a frontage that could hardly fail to attract the attention of passers-by.

By Easter 1883 all the alterations were complete, and four months later Jesse established the business as a private company, Boot and Company Limited, with himself as chairman and managing director. His new shop was attracting customers not only from all over Nottingham but also from distant villages and country towns. Business reached a peak on Saturdays when all the staff continued to work until late into the evening. Some idea of the busy routine is captured by Bob Elliott, who joined Jesse as an errand boy in 1881, and who wrote down his memoirs of those days in a 1933 issue of the *Beacon,* Boots house magazine for non-retail staff.

'In anticipation of the rush on Saturdays, there was a good supply of everything that could be weighed up in the quantities expected to be sold, this work occupying the spare time throughout the week and

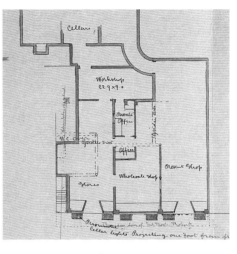

Ground floor plan of the new Goose Gate shop, 1881.

When Jesse's new shop opened, in 1884, it dazzled customers with its sheer size and its spectacular window displays.

Jesse in his early thirties.

Whenever possible Jesse bought goods cheaply, in bulk, in order to sell them at greatly reduced prices to his customers. He once bought a huge quantity of Epsom Salts, selling them at 1d a pound instead of the usual ½d an ounce. For several weeks the shop assistants were rushed off their feet, weighing and packaging the salts to keep pace with demand.

being participated in by all the counter men. There were some lines, though, which were not packed more than a few hours before selling and these, when big lines, were rather a bother. Three such lines which we used to sell in enormous quantities in the hot weather were 'Boiling' Magnesia, Saline and Lemon Kali, which were located on the grocery side of the shop.

Eight o'clock was the time for opening the shop and within a few minutes of that hour all the assistants had arrived. With the smallest time possible given to 'dusting', etc, the assistants on this side of the shop took off their coats and started to 'weigh up' these articles in ¼lbs, ½lbs, etc, working at their fastest: by about 10.15 there would be stacks of these things sufficient to last until the evening. So the day started with two hours' hard work preliminary to the rush of customers. The assistants would then put on their coats and clean white aprons, ready for the fray. By that time customers would be coming in a steady stream. From 10.30 to 12 most of the village carriers would come with their general orders to be assembled ready for the carriers calling later, or to be sent to their carts. Between 10.30 and 12.30 the 'swell' shoppers arrived in large numbers, using horse-drawn carriages where now they use motor cars.

There would be a good sprinkling of farmers and that type of customer, also town people, making a crowd which filled the shop until about 12.30. From 12.30 to about two o'clock business was a bit quieter, not enough to allow the staff to leave the shop for a mid-day meal, but enough to allow them to get something to eat on the premises in relays. Then, on again, busier than ever - mostly with visitors to the town - up to about four o'clock or a little later. Then came the quietest part of the day, when staff could leave the shop in batches for three-quarters of an hour, which meant the chance for a substantial meal and so ready for the evening's rush, which was as fierce as anything during the day and comprised mostly town people. By nine o'clock things were quieter, but certainly (busy) enough for the tired assistants. When closing time came at 10 or 10.30 the most pleasing thought was that the next day was Sunday!'

The most striking feature of the new Goose Gate shop was its spectacular displays. Sometimes the whole window area would be made up of displays of a single product. In his article in the *Beacon*, Bob Elliott recalled when the windows of both floors were filled with nothing but Seltzogenes, which were used to make fizzy drinks...

'The display was so striking that it was almost impossible for anyone to pass without seeing it. I forget the prices, but think the three-pint size was perhaps 7s 11d and the five-pint 11s 6d. A seltzogene was a new thing to most people, but as a result of that display we sold a great many of the three-pint and five-pint and some of the eight-pint sizes, and created a steady demand for the charges.'

On another occasion he filled the windows with nothing but sponges, then sent out telegrams to 200 wealthy residents, inviting them to 'come and see our great sponge display', an ingenious idea which took advantage of a Post Office reduction in the price of a telegram from a shilling to sixpence. One telegram was sent to a leading manufacturer at his house in the affluent Park area; then, on discovering that he was 'out of town', a groom was despatched to take the telegram to his country residence. However, on having his privacy disturbed, the gentleman concerned flew into a rage, immediately saddled up his horse and rode into Nottingham to make a personal complaint to Jesse. On arriving at the shop he was in a thoroughly bad temper, but Jesse and his assistants quickly managed to calm him down and within only a few minutes he was leaving the shop, with a proud smile on his face and carrying an armful of sponges!

One of the shop's pioneering attractions was its hydraulic passenger lift installed after additional sales rooms had been opened at Goose Gate on the first floor. The lift was beautifully fitted out and ran so smoothly that passengers could scarcely detect any movement at all as they travelled up and down the building. But, such a device had not been seen before in Nottingham and many customers were reluctant to use it, preferring instead to use the stairs. Not to be outdone, Jesse hired an assistant to operate the lift and to assure customers that the lift would do them no harm!

A seltzogene, used for making fizzy drinks. Jesse once filled the whole **Goose Gate** window with nothing but seltzogenes, one of his most popular household lines.

Tempted by a succession of bargains and eye-catching displays the public flocked to Jesse's Goose Gate store. To keep pace with demand he was now employing ten 'indoor staff', two porters and an errand boy; and takings were rising with every week that passed. For most businessmen the Goose Gate shop would have been an end in itself, but for Jesse it was only a beginning.

JESSE
BRANCHES
OUT

7 London Road

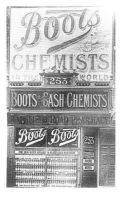

253 Mansfield Road

Looking northwards up Mansfield Road, one of the town's busiest streets. A Boots store once occupied the corner of Mansfield Road and Shakespeare Street (on the left of the photograph).

WITH THE GOOSE GATE shop well established and sales at £28,000 a year Jesse's thoughts turned to plans for expansion. Why not use the same ideas that had proved such a success at Goose Gate in other parts of Nottingham? He had the business experience, the financial backing, a genius for sales and the dedication, if only he could keep up the exhausting routine necessary to see it through. He decided to go ahead and did so with remarkable speed, buying up vacant properties all over Nottingham and refurbishing them in characteristic style. Often he chose sites in poorer districts, like Hockley, where properties were reasonably cheap and where local residents were in urgent need of herbs and medicines. Stores were opened on Alfreton Road in Radford, on Arkwright Street in the Meadows at 7 London Road, 253 Mansfield Road, and on the corner of Shakespeare Street and Mansfield Road.

Jesse had a particular talent for attracting publicity for his shops. To promote sales of 'Soft Soap' at the Goose Gate store he once placed wooden tubs, piled high with soap at greatly reduced prices, in the window area and every so often two men would appear by the tubs, studiously weighing and wrapping the soap in neatly labelled parcels. He once caused a sensation when, on managing to secure an enormous quantity of tinned salmon he sold it at nearly half its usual price, 4½d instead of 8d at the Goose Gate shop. In Hockley the possibility of buying salmon had always been remote, but now it was suddenly within their reach. As people queued up to buy their tins they asked time and again, "will you open it?" as few families in Hockley had such a device as a tin opener. Jesse obliged by asking one of his porters to open the tins as they were removed from the cases, though his fingers soon ached with the task as he struggled to keep pace with the endless queue of customers. On one Saturday morning the shop sold no fewer than 40 cases of salmon, which amounted to a staggering 1,440 individual tins.

Wherever Jesse opened a new shop, it instantly became a feature of the neighbourhood. Everyone talked about the latest bargains and offers, everyone went to see the latest window displays and everyone talked about Jesse Boot. He had become a personality of Nottingham.

Confident of his position and reputation in Nottingham, Jesse began to look at the possibility of branches in other towns. From his father, Jesse had inherited a wide circle of retail contacts all over the Midlands and North, and he had always been careful to preserve and extend this side of the business. Regular deliveries from the Goose Gate wholesale department were made by travelling salesmen using horse drawn carts, though with the dawn of the railway age Jesse was able to consider a much larger scale operation. As the Victorian railway network spread over England, it not only transformed the landscape, as an army of navvies dug tunnels and threw up embankments, but also drew yet more people into towns like Nottingham, further encouraging commerce and industry. With good communications from Nottingham, by road and rail,

Jesse was able to open branches much further afield. It meant still more work, but he knew the time was right, and in October 1884, he opened his first branch outside Nottingham, at Snig Hill in Sheffield, which proved a resounding success. Jesse had done it again.

Then, shortly afterwards, he opened yet another shop, on the High Street in Lincoln, and other shops elsewhere soon followed.

Railway navvies take a break from their work on the Nottingham Surburban line to pose for a photograph. Nottingham's railways played a vital role in the town's industrial development.

Snig Hill, Sheffield, the first Boots branch to be opened outside Nottingham.

Arkwright Street

Edwin Waring, who Jesse appointed to manage the dispensing side of the business.

Jesse opened every new shop to a fanfare of publicity. To check that all the necessary arrangements had been made for an opening he liked to visit each new shop, travelling on horseback and sleeping overnight in the shop itself. First thing in the morning he fussed over stock displays and counter layouts, and ran a critical eye over the staff to make sure they were all neatly turned out. Before an opening numerous advertisements were placed in newspapers and hundreds of publicity leaflets were distributed to local householders. Sometimes a gaily decorated carriage, covered in posters, was paraded up and down the local streets. On the opening day a brass band was often engaged to help attract a crowd and one of Jesse's staff would stand outside the shop, ringing a bell and announcing the latest price reductions in a booming voice. All the shop windows would be crammed full of bargains and large signs would advertise Boots 'Reformed Prices'.

Sales at Jesse's branches were never better but his very success had provoked a hostile reaction from many fellow chemists and druggists. They openly criticised his cut-price tactics and even tried to cast doubt on some of his products. To counter such criticisms and help build up public confidence in his products as pure and natural Jesse retitled the business, Boots Pure Drug Company. Some of Jesse's competitors also claimed that only traditional chemists, and not general stores or large companies, should have the legal right to dispense medicines, even after the House of Lords, in 1879, ruled that such a view could not be supported in law. The ruling did, however, make it clear that anyone who dispensed medicines had to be a qualified chemist. As Jesse wanted all his stores to offer dispensing services he set about finding a first class chemist to run a new dispensary at Goose Gate and oversee the appointment of chemists in the other branches.

Jesse looked far and wide for the right man, eventually discovering Edwin Waring, an ideal choice, at a high class chemists on Market Street, in Nottingham.

A typical Boots dispensary of the Victorian period.

Waring was a 'typically old fashioned chemist' who had built up a solid professional reputation, especially among the well-to-do. Jesse had to use all his persuasive powers to entice him to the working class district of Hockley, but it was worth the effort. Waring brought with him just the prestige that Jesse needed, and his pleasant personality and willingness to accept Jesse's progressive business methods proved an invaluable asset. Not long after his appointment Waring halved the cost of prescriptions and ensured that all items sold were attractively packaged. He also worked hard to establish dispensaries in Boots growing number of branches and helped Jesse to find the best staff possible. Waring was capable of attracting just the right kind of chemists into the new branches, men who inspired confidence and trust in their customers; and he kept a close eye on their work and progress.

Another key figure in Jesse's plans for expansion was Albert Thompson, who started at Goose Gate as a junior retail assistant at the age of 21. Albert rose by a combination of application and practical ability to the position of General Manager. For the first few years of his employment Albert lodged with Jesse, Mary and Jane, above the shop, becoming a close friend of the whole family.

Jesse was now working a sixteen-hour day. Every night after the Goose Gate shop closed he worked on, checking the stock and going over accounts. In his own words it was a life of 'drudgery and monotony', involving hours and hours of painstaking work:

'I was busy behind the counter, but my day did not end with the closing of the shop, for I had hours of writing to do. Later on, when there were several branches, I would work right through the night for a fortnight at stock-taking'.

A Boots delivery cart

Narrow Marsh, on the south side of Nottingham, was one of the town's worst slum areas. This photograph was taken in 1913 shortly before a large part of the area was demolished.

The Forest, one of Nottingham's largest public parks.

There were few opportunities to get away from the world of work, but on Sundays, after attending chapel, he would often take a stroll alongside the River Trent or in one of the local parks, pausing occasionally to chat to friends or listen to the music of a brass band. For anyone trapped in the sunless streets of Hockley, Narrow Marsh or Broad Marsh, the council parks provided a rare opportunity to breathe fresh air, see flowers and trees and take some gentle exercise away from the crashing noise of giant lace machines and snapping factory supervisors. Jesse recognised that Nottingham's parks and open spaces were of immense value, not only to himself, but to all local people, and in later years he was to repay his appreciation of their existence by donating large areas of land to the Council for the creation of several new parks, each beautifully laid out and maintained at Jesse's own expense.

On Bank Holidays Jesse liked to go on long, solitary walks in Derbyshire, especially in the Peak District, where his favourite spot was Dovedale. As his friendship with Albert Thompson grew, the two men often set off on walks together, Jesse reminiscing about earlier days when, as a young boy, he helped to gather herbs for the shop. For a time they explored the countryside on bicycles and they even tried out a tandem that Jesse had spotted in a local shop window. Unable to resist the new-fangled device he bought it there and then and insisted that he and Albert give it a trial run straight away. On these expeditions Jesse could relax and discuss his problems with a sympathetic friend, go over his plans for new branches and share his hopes for the future.

But these occasional days in the sunshine could not disguise the fact that Jesse's long hours in the shop were taking their toll on his health. His family and friends urged him to take things more easily, but in the summer of 1885 he suffered a complete breakdown. Overtired and drained of energy he lacked any will to go on. He even considered selling the company, remarking towards the end of his life that: 'My health suffered so much and I was so worn out that at thirty-six anybody could have had my business very cheap'.

Before making a final decision Jesse was persuaded by his sister, Jane, to take a holiday in Jersey. Its scenery, seclusion and warm climate proved ideal. Away from the worries of running the company he began to relax for the first time in years. In search of company he followed up several contacts suggested by Jane, who had herself spent a holiday in Jersey. At a small Methodist chapel in St. Helier he was introduced to Florence Rowe, the 23 year old daughter of William Rowe, who ran a bookshop and stationers in St. Helier's main shopping street. Florence's bright, vivacious personality immediately captured Jesse's attention and a holiday romance soon blossomed. She had a wide circle of friends, loved entertaining and took a lively interest in art and fashion, in contrast to Jesse whose life had revolved around a narrow world of business, and his immediate family and chapel friends. The couple complemented each other perfectly, and they married in the summer of the following year. John, their first child was born on the 19 January 1889 followed by a second son Laurie who died in infancy and daughters Dorothy and Margery.

Jesse and his sister, Jane. It was Jane who urged Jesse to take a holiday on Jersey when he became ill from overwork.

194 JERSEY. — La Vallée de Saint-Pierre. — St-Peter's Valley. — LL.

Jersey Island where, during a recuperative holiday in the summer of 1885, Jesse met his future wife, Florence Rowe. Florence was the daughter of William Rowe who owned a bookshop and stationers in St Helier.

Jesse and Florence at the time of their marriage in 1886.

The children: John,
Dorothy and Margery.

The marriage rejuvenated Jesse's enthusiasm for life and for the company. All thoughts of selling-out had been dispelled and he returned to work with renewed vigour.

With the dedicated support of Edwin Waring and Albert Thompson, Jesse started to plan yet more branches. In customary style he opened one new branch after another, concentrating on Nottingham and Sheffield, where he was already well-established, but also extending into other towns in the East Midlands. Florence, too, began to take an increasing interest in the company. Drawing on her knowledge of the Rowe's family shop in St. Helier, Florence began to introduce a whole range of new lines at Goose Gate - books, stationery, fancy goods, artists' materials and picture frames. The success of this venture led Jesse and Florence to develop a concept of Boots shops, not just as pharmacies but as department stores.

In 1891, when Jesse secured the leasehold on a property at the corner of High Street and Pelham Street, it presented Jesse and Florence with an ideal opportunity to incorporate all their latest retail ideas. It also had the advantage of taking Jesse into the very heart of the town centre, which was rapidly developing as one of the most fashionable commercial centres in the Midlands. Around the Exchange, where the Council held its meetings, and the Market Place, were rows of elegant shops, all competing with each other to be bigger and better.

On acquiring the Pelham Street site Jesse decided to demolish most of the existing building and rebuild it in a style that would match anything else to be seen in Nottingham at that time. The new shop was breathtaking. Florence's artistic flare was evident at every turn. On the ground floor there were entire departments for toiletries, books, stationery and perfumes, all laid out on attractive mahogany counters that had been purpose-built by Jesse's own team of joiners and carpenters. In addition there was a dispensary that was unrivalled in the range of medicines it could provide and in the skill of its chemists. Above the ground floor there was an ornate gallery, supported by a colonnade of cast-iron pillars, where pictures, all chosen by Florence, were hung in artistic arrangements, and where enticing displays of decorative glass and fancy goods tempted shoppers to spend yet more money after they had visited the main shop area. Taking advantage of the new invention of

In 1892 Jesse opened a new shop at a prime town centre site on the corner of Pelham Street and High Street. Its elegance, style and lavish displays soon became the 'talk-of-the-town'.

The Fancy Department at Pelham Street. As well as contributing to the store's interior design, Florence herself introduced many of the new lines at Pelham Street, including fancy goods, pictures and decorative glass.

Tower, Pelham Street

electricity, Jesse installed a power generator in the store so that during the long winter evenings enthralled shoppers were bathed in the light cast by 12 arc lamps, each of 2,000 candle power. Skylights inserted along the whole length of the roof allowed yet more light into the store to further illuminate the displays. By combining their mutual talents, Jesse and Florence had produced a shop that had become the 'talk of the town'. And more than that it was to become the model for future Boots department stores throughout the country.

In 1903 the whole Pelham Street shop was re-modelled by local architect, Albert Nelson Bromley, who Jesse commissioned to design many of Boots branches up until the late 1920s. Pelham Street became a 'model' for future Boots department stores throughout the country. In this photograph, staff pose in front of the new store, with its fine Art Nouveau style windows.

LARGEST,
BEST AND
CHEAPEST

AS JESSE'S RETAIL EMPIRE began to grow, the Goose Gate shop became more and more cramped. As well as being one of Boots busiest shops it had become the centre of all Jesse's wholesale and manufacturing activities, and it served as an office for Jesse himself. In the three small cottages at the back of the shop, his assistants did their best to keep up with the non-stop demands of the branches for bronchial lozenges, lobelia pills, syrups, ointments, packets of herbs, influenza mixture, vapour rubs and many more lines, with new ones being added by Jesse all the time. They weighed, measured, concocted, bottled and boxed hundreds of products every day.

In 1885 Jesse had engaged a Mr Holthouse to build up the manufacturing side of the company. Holthouse had previously been with a leading manufacturing chemist in Hull but Jesse persuaded him that his future lay with Boots. Goose Gate was a hive of activity, but Jesse and Holthouse quickly concluded that it was far too small. There were piles of sacks, packets, boxes, bottles and cases everywhere, with assistants falling over each other in their efforts to meet deadlines for orders.

Jesse urgently needed to find larger premises for wholesale and manufacturing staff. He wanted Boots to be fully self-contained so that he could control not only prices but also the quality of every product sold in his shops. He wanted to sell and develop new product lines, to print all his own publicity literature, to design and build all his own shops, to run his own transport fleet and even to frame all the pictures sold in Boots shops. He wanted to be the 'Largest, Best and Cheapest' chemist in the whole country.

By considering such a huge step forward, while continuing to open new branches, Jesse was putting himself under considerable strain. Suffering from near total exhaustion he had to retreat to bed for days at a time, and worse still he began to suffer from occasional bouts of rheumatoid arthritis, a crippling illness that caused him constant pain. Yet he worked on regardless, as determined as ever to build up the company. After a long search for suitable premises all over Nottingham, he eventually took out a lease on three large rooms that had become available in Elliott's lace factory on Island Street, not far from Hockley.

Island Street ran along the centre of a virtual island formed by the Nottingham canal basin. The local streets were a hotch-potch of factories, workshops and grimy terraces, though for Jesse there was the tempting prospect of cheap land and property. Running down the west side of Island Street was London Road, a main road southwards out of Nottingham. On the other side of London Road, opposite Island Street, sat another area, also ripe for development, that included Parkinson Street and Station Street, which Jesse also had his eye on.

Mr H B Holthouse, a manufacturing chemist, who was employed by Jesse to develop pharmaceutical production. At first he worked in a row of small cottages at the back of the Goose Gate store, but after the move to Island Street he built up an entire manufacturing department.

Boots Island Street works (from an insurance plan of 1892). When Goose Gate became overcrowded Jesse began to look for larger premises for the wholesale and manufacturing side of the business. Eventually he moved into Island Street, a hotch-potch of factories, warehouses, small industrial workshops and grimy terraces. It was a dingy part of the town but land and property were cheap, and Jesse was soon buying up the whole area. It was also convenient for the Nottingham Canal and the local railway network.

Tablet production
at Island Street.

Exterior of Boots
Steam Printing at
Island Street where an
endless supply of
labels, advertising
circulars and posters
was turned out for the
company.

As always Jesse was thinking of his company's future needs. No sooner had Jesse transferred Mr Holthouse to Island Street, with his gigantic boiling pans, percolators and tincture presses, than he was renting additional rooms in the factory, extending into adjoining buildings and buying up surrounding houses to replace them soon afterwards with his own buildings. Every step of the work was supervised by Jesse himself, despite his poor state of health, with nothing left to chance. While in some ways Jesse's concern for detail was admirable his reluctance to delegate work greatly aggravated his declining state of health. He rarely, if ever, relaxed. So the work went on, at a furious pace. By the end of 1892 Jesse had taken over the whole of Elliott's former lace factory, and had further properties around Island Street and on Parkinson Street and Station Street. At the Island Street works, as the whole group of buildings became known, he was then employing at least 80 staff engaged in packing, bottling, shop fitting, printing, advertising, picture framing, laboratory work, transport, and accounts. In 1892 Island Street was highlighted in *Nottingham Illustrated: Its Arts, Trade and Commerce.* The feature provides a unique glimpse of Jesse's manufacturing empire. Arriving in the drug department, the writer noted:

'Long ranges of bins and shelves are stocked with jars, tins, huge earthenware vessels, carboys and bottles, all filled with drugs of various kinds, but all systematically arranged, plainly labelled, and ease of access. Further on we see large barrels, casks, vats, etc; containing Citric and Tartaric Acid, Camphor, Quinine, Magnesia, Gum Arabic, and many other similar articles'.

Then, at the patent medicine department ...

'Immense quantities of all the proprietary articles, many of them of world-wide notoriety, are to be seen; indeed there will not be found one article wanting of all the advertised specifics for the ills that flesh is heir to. We notice Clarke's Blood Mixture, Frazer's Tablets, Jacob's Oil, Chlorodyne, Liver and Indigestion Pills and Mixtures, Children's Soothing and Rheumatic Pills, Mixtures and Lotions; Anti-stiff, Mackenzie's Catarrh Smelling Bottles, Towle's Pills, Hair Restorers, Nervines, Fenning's Children's Medicines, Boots Composition Powders, Quinine Wine, Doctor Armstrong's Quinine and Iron Tonics, and a host of others, all good in their way, and each highly appreciated by those who have obtained relief and comfort by its use.'

Specially equipped areas had been laid out for mixing chemicals, manufacturing pills and drying herbs and powders. Any necessary steam power to drive machinery came from a 200 hp engine and two boilers that had been installed in a nearby outbuilding.

Campbells Cherry Cough Cure

An early photograph of staff in the Packing Room.

A large proportion of Jesse's staff was female. As he watched the women and girls arriving each day at Island Street, it must have brought back memories of younger days when he had watched a similar invasion of female workers hurrying into the Lace Market. In the bottling stores it was mainly girls who stood over an endless procession of bottles which had to be washed, filled, and corked, non-stop, day-in, day-out. In the packing department groups of women and girls worked at incredible speed to stick labels onto every size and shape of container imaginable and to pack up the bottles and boxes ready for transport.

Bottling at Island Street. This work was done entirely by women and girls who washed, filled, corked and labelled an endless procession of bottles.

Everywhere, workmen with handbarrows darted to and fro shifting stacks of bottles and boxes, while a steam hoist and hydraulic lift were used to move goods between floors. To print labels and to produce handbills and posters for Boots shops a printing room was set-up with five steam printing machines, presses and a guillotine. Other rooms were occupied by shopfitters, painters, accounts clerks and, to supervise the whole enterprise, Jesse himself moved into a private office immediately above the packing department, linked to all his main branches by 'telephonic communication'.

Here Jesse sat at what had become the heart of Boots Pure Drug Company. Here he could liaise directly with Albert Thompson, work on his plans for new shops, check the accounts at a moment's notice and keep a daily check on his workforce. Jesse kept a close eye on every aspect of work, down to the last detail.

A female employee in the packing department once recalled how he complained about the amount of string being used for wrapping parcels…"if we cut the string on the parcels too long, we get pulled up for it". She also recalled his passion for timekeeping. At Island Street he introduced a new invention known as a 'patent timekeeper and clock' to record the comings and goings of every employee.

In choosing Island Street for his wholesale and manufacturing base, Jesse was aware of its huge potential for developing the company's transport system. Its location alongside the Nottingham Canal meant that a regular supply of coal for Island Street's engine house could be brought in on barges that passed through a string of colliery towns along the canal's route from Nottingham to Langley Mill, in Derbyshire. The Boots fleet consisted of two petrol-driven boats, the Thistle and Marworth, each with sleeping and living quarters, and eight unpowered barges which could each carry 60 tons of coal. A round trip for a single boat and its barge plying between Langley Mill and Nottingham took two days to complete and involved a total of 18 locks each way. Island Street was also ideally located to benefit from its position near a network of railway sidings and goods sheds just to the south of the canal. Nor was Island Street far from either the London Road Great Northern Railway Station or the Midland Station, on Station Street, where Jesse acquired more property in the 1890s.

Coal picking at Clifton Colliery around 1895. To supplement delivery of coal by barge, regular journeys were made to Clifton and Watnall pits by horse-drawn carts to collect coal for Island Street.

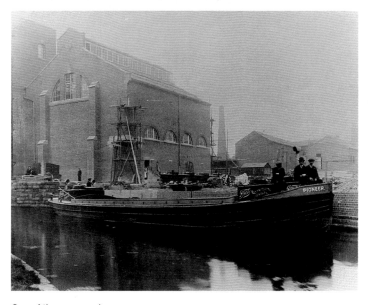

One of the company's barges on the Nottingham Canal. The barges kept Island Street's engine house supplied with coal from pits that lay along the canal's route through Nottinghamshire and Derbyshire.

Horses were, up until the First World War, at the heart of Boots road transport section. They were the company's pride and joy, and were shown regularly at agricultural shows.

Equally important was road transport. From the 1880s Jesse employed seven men, five horses, four vans, two carts and a dray to move raw materials and keep branches regularly supplied with stock. When Nottingham Corporation Tramways dropped their horse-drawn trams, after electrification in 1904-5, Jesse bought six of their horses to help with branch deliveries and to transport coal from Clifton and Watnall pits. In the summer, after a long day's work, the horses were walked up and down Parkinson Street to cool down for half an hour before returning to their stables for the night. The horses were the pride of the company. They were kept in perfect condition and were much admired, winning countless prizes and trophies up and down the country.

With his own manufacturing works, distribution and transport system well established, Jesse found a new, and even larger, appetite for expansion. By 1893 Jesse had opened 33 shops, including seven branches in Nottingham, and with Island Street working flat out, there seemed to be no limit to the company's growth. In fact scarcely a week seemed to pass without a branch opening somewhere in the country. He began to open shops further south, in Peterborough, Bedford and Wellingborough; in East Anglia; in fashionable seaside resorts; and in the West Midlands, where in Birmingham he opened an unbelievable nine branches in a single year.

At the turn of the century Jesse owned more than 250 shops in a retail chain that far outstripped any rival. All over his shops, in large letters, and in advertisements he could now proudly claim to be the 'Largest, Best and Cheapest' chemist in town.

A FAMILY,
A BUSINESS
AND AN
EMPIRE

In the early 1900s Jesse began to take out whole page advertisements in the national press.

Nottingham was granted city status by this charter from Queen Victoria in 1897.

IN 1898 JESSE MOVED from makeshift offices at Island Street into several rooms that had become vacant in Hine & Mundella's hosiery factory on Station Street. The building's impressive size and handsome proportions were very much in keeping with Jesse's rising commercial status and he gradually bought up the whole factory to adapt as the company's head office.

From his new offices at Station Street Jesse began to transform Boots into a business empire. In addition to opening new branches he started to take over existing chemists, including William Day's Southern Drug Company, a pharmaceutical retail chain of 60 stores in London and the South of England. Eager to promote his new position Jesse began a major advertising campaign, taking whole page adverts in the *Times* and *Daily Mail* during the Christmas of 1904 and launching similar campaigns in provincial newspapers.

Back home, the people of Nottingham watched Jesse's progress with fascination and pride. Nottingham was a hard working town that respected effort, invention and enterprise. In 1897 its own progress had been recognised by a royal charter, granted by Queen Victoria, giving Nottingham city status. It was a go-ahead city full of energy and ideas and it was producing a wealth of industrialists, who, like Jesse, were determined to make their way in the world. Among them was John Player, whose giant tobacco empire, founded on the popularity of such brands as 'Navy Cut', began in 1877 when he bought a small tobacco factory in Nottingham's back streets.

Interior, the Raleigh Cycle Company, founded by Frank Bowden in the 1880s. Raleigh was producing 10,000 bicycles a year by the turn of the century.

Equally successful was the founder of Nottingham's Raleigh Cycle Company, Frank Bowden, who was manufacturing 10,000 cycles a year by 1900, many of them for sale abroad. Yet despite his fame and fortune Jesse continued to live a simple life, working as hard as ever, allowing himself few breaks or holidays. In fact his punishing routine was becoming a major concern to close friends and members of the family. A combination of overwork and fatigue sometimes made him short tempered and his arthritis obliged him to spend much of the day confined to a wheelchair. For Jesse, who had once enjoyed long walks, cycling and other outdoor pursuits, it must have been intensely frustrating to have become so immobile, but he rarely, if ever, complained.

Jesse's continuing commitment to his life and work owed a great deal to Florence, whose own love of life prevented Jesse from becoming too inward looking or depressed. She also contributed lots of creative ideas to the company's development, using her artistic skills and interests in the designing of new stores. Together they planned every detail of new shop facades, interior fittings and decoration. Every store was designed to be a local landmark where shopping was to be not just a chore but an experience. They were especially fond of revival Gothic and Tudor styles and would lavish money on the creation of period-piece reconstructions that became architectural focal points in towns all over Britain. Some stores incorporated fine Art Nouveau features that drew on the contemporary influence of the Arts and Crafts movement. Much of the basic architectural work was undertaken by Albert Nelson Bromley, a Nottingham architect, whose first commission for Boots was alterations and additions to buildings at Island Street in 1895. Decorative additions were largely the work of Morley Horder, who specialised in stained glass windows, statues and other design features that often portrayed local historical figures.

Boots Trent Bridge store was built in a Tudor style much favoured by Jesse and Florence. It included a Book Lovers Library and a café.

A typical Book Lovers Library interior of the early 1900s. The idea for the libraries came from Florence, who took a great interest in literature and the arts. The interiors reflected Florence's interest in design.

Library tokens

Florence's interest in literature and the arts inspired her to found the Boots Book Lovers Library. For only sixpence a title borrowers could make a selection from collections of 'safe' novels, biographies and travel books - any provocative stories were carefully identified with a red label on the spine to alert more sensitive subscribers to their contents. As the libraries were located at the back of shops or on upstairs floors they also encouraged sales as subscribers were obliged to make their way through the main sales areas with all their tempting displays. By 1903 libraries had been established in 193 branches, and by the mid-1930s, when the scheme was at its height, the number had grown to 450, with well over half a million subscribers.

Another idea, also fostered by Florence, was to open elegantly furnished cafés in Boots larger stores. These attracted the fashionable middle classes to shop at Boots, making their visits something of a social occasion and encouraging them to build up a loyalty to the company. The décor of every café was chosen personally by Florence herself and she insisted on selecting the chinaware, the furnishings and style of lighting. Following the success of Boots first café, in Brighton on the south coast, a much larger café was opened at the Pelham Street store, in Nottingham. Jesse noted, with evident pride, that 'Ours was the first departmental establishment to introduce to Nottingham this innovation, so popular in London and New York'. Though the introduction of libraries and cafés had only a limited impact on sales, they proved invaluable in raising the image of Boots shops and in the longer term they brought in a more affluent class of shopper.

Although Jesse and Florence were both totally absorbed in developing the company they were also devoted to their family, treasuring every moment with their children that time would allow. For a time Jesse and Florence lived at Carlyle House, a modest villa on Burns Street, near the Arboretum. Then, in search of more space for their growing family, they moved to a much larger house in the Park district of Nottingham. They called their new home, St. Helier, in affectionate memory of their first meeting on Jersey.

With all her usual zest, style and sense of fashion, Florence immediately set about decorating the house, achieving a richness and warmth that was a world away from Jesse's early days in Goose Gate. For Jesse, St. Helier was a comfortable retreat where he could relax with his family and share with Florence in hosting a convivial round of dinners and social gatherings. At the hub of it all was Florence, whose outgoing personality and refined taste for art, music, books and fashion attracted a constant stream of guests from all walks of life. In later years, when Jesse became President of the Nottingham Liberal Association, they hosted visits from many distinguished Liberal politicians of the day, including Asquith and Herbert Samuel.

Elegant cafés, furnished and decorated with characteristic flair by Florence, attracted even more customers into Boots stores.

The Park, Nottingham, a district of spacious villas, large gardens and tree-lined streets was developed near the Castle by the Duke of Newcastle during the 19th century.

Jesse, Florence and the Liberal politician, Herbert Samuel MP at 'St. Helier' (Jesse's house in the Park).

On summer days hundreds of people enjoyed walking along the banks of the River Trent, taking boat trips down the river or simply watching the world go by for an hour or two. In the background is the Midland Industrial Exhibition, which was destroyed by fire in 1904.

Boots staff enjoy a trip to Derbyshire on 6 August 1894.

No less important to Jesse and Florence than their home and family was the welfare of their hundreds of staff. Jesse's concern for industrial welfare had been inspired by the writings of the Quaker, Joseph Rowntree, and he much admired the work of Cadbury, who had created a 'model' community at Bournville. With Florence's help he began to introduce a whole range of philanthropic ideas to improve the lot of Boots employees. One of their most popular ideas was to organise staff outings to local beauty spots or to the seaside. In the summer Jesse and Florence hired charabancs to take staff on excursions for a day in the countryside, to places like Hazelford Ferry, by the River Trent, or the fields at Plumtree. After the excitement of the journey, a hearty picnic was followed by a leisurely stroll, or, for the younger ones, there were organised sports and games. In time these excursions became more adventurous. On the 6 August 1894 a special train took staff to Castleton, in Jesse's beloved Derbyshire. The journey was eagerly anticipated in a souvenir brochure:

'Many pictures of rural felicity in pretty homes and cottages may be glanced at as we go by, whilst at one point, if the day be clear, a long stretch of country will show us as far as Crich Stand, by Matlock. But the most frequent feature is the pit head and the blasting furnace, reminding us of the busy everyday life which we are leaving behind for a day of leisure and enjoyment. What is this that heaves in sight? A deformed church - by all that's curious - Chesterfield to wit - with its crooked spire - reminds us of a corkscrew - and by association of ideas, that we are thirsty. Out with the lemonade!'

At Castleton a visit to its renowned caverns cast a 'spell of awe' on the visitors who advanced by ropewalk into the mouth of the Great Peak Cavern to savour 'a weird and uncanny silence'. In 1902 a trip to Skegness was organised by Florence for the 'Lady Clerks and Nottingham Warehouse Staffs'. On arrival it was suggested that 'a visit to the beach and pier may very well occupy the time before dinner'. At 12 noon a slap-up meal of roast beef, apple pie and jellies and cream was served in the Pavilion, followed in the afternoon by entertainment from a band of pierrots. On a trip to the Franco-British Exhibition in July 1908 Boots staff joined excited queues to enter the illuminated Hong Kong puzzle house in which 'the visitor finds himself in a revolving cylinder, and on leaving is entirely at a loss to know where he is'. Even braver souls could sample the breathtaking delights of elevated 'car' rides like the Spiral or Canadian Toboggan or try the 'sensational' Flip Flap that took its wide-eyed passengers 200 feet into mid-air.

The role of Florence in encouraging welfare initiatives, especially for female staff, cannot be underestimated. She came to regard the problems of her own 'Dear Girls', whether they served behind shop counters or worked in one of Boots factories or warehouses, as a matter of personal concern. On discovering that many of the Island Street girls were arriving at the works without having had

Programme for the Franco-British Exhibition, London, in July 1908. Boots staff travelled to the exhibition on two special trains chartered by the company for the day.

The canteen, Island Street, which was originally introduced by Florence.

Florence was especially concerned with the welfare of female staff. These silk banners were sent at Christmas to women and girls in appreciation for their work and to provide spiritual comfort.

any breakfast she insisted that from that day onwards they were all to be given a cup of steaming hot cocoa first thing in the morning. Every Christmas she sent a silk banner, printed with a moral verse, to female staff in special appreciation for their work and to help support them through any difficulties that might arise in the year to come. Sometimes Florence visited the girls in their homes at times of special hardship or during long illnesses and she would travel any distance to help sort out a problem faced by one of her shop girls in the branches.

Florence's particular concern for the shop girls was rooted in her own memories of serving behind the counter of her father's shop on Jersey; and she never missed an opportunity to reassure them that she always had their best interests at heart. A letter, written by Florence in 1913, underlines her commitment to the female shop staff:

THE PARK, NOTTINGHAM.
Sept. 21st, (19)13

My Dear Girls,
Lest any of you should think that because I have taken up the cause of the College girl, you may be in any danger of losing your position or salary I want to assure you that such will not be the case. You will be more studied in the future than in the past not less, and your salaries will be raised rather than lowered. I want to help all girls, to whatever class they belong, to help each other and to help themselves. Most of you know that I know quite well what shop life is, for I can never remember the time when I was not in one. My earliest recollections are of toddling round the

counters at my father's side and learning from him that all labour was dignified and that to be courteous and obliging was a great asset in the business world and that life in a shop could be and ought to be a high calling. Because I think of him, one of the good old fashioned booksellers of a past generation, who taught me all that I ever knew that is worth remembering and because I left school at fourteen just as most of you have done there is no reason why we cannot learn something from those who have had all sorts of advantages in learning that neither you nor I have had; rest assured that you will always have my first care and consideration and that whatever efforts I have made in the past to help you will be more than doubled in the future.

Always your sincere friend and well wisher,
Florence Boot

For many years Florence was assisted in her pioneering schemes by Eleanor Kelly, a young welfare worker who had spent a week at Bournville to observe their welfare activities, before starting at Boots. Eleanor's appointment was itself a pioneering move, as few companies at that time engaged welfare staff, but with Florence's support she was able to make considerable progress. In no time she had renovated the works' canteen, introduced home visiting schemes and established a sick room, attended by nurses and a part-time doctor.

In about 1900 Jesse built a delightful summer house, known as Plaisaunce, in a park on the south bank of the River Trent near Trent Bridge. It was not only large enough to accommodate Jesse and the family at weekends in the summer, but it also had a dance hall and elegant tea rooms furnished in immaculate style by Florence. Jesse began to spend more and more time at Plaisaunce. Now racked with pain from arthritis he would have his wheelchair placed on the balcony so that he could gaze over the River Trent and country meadows and find, at least for a few minutes, a sense of peace and relaxation.

Around Plaisaunce, tennis courts and sports grounds were laid out for a growing number of Boots teams that began to compete on a county-wide basis. On long sunny afternoons refreshments were served to thirsty participants in tennis matches, athletics events and swimming galas. For Florence, Plaisaunce was ideal for treating her 'girls' to tea parties and musical concerts; after which Florence always asked the girls to join with her in singing a hymn. Then the girls were all taken home in a fleet of horse drawn buggies. For all the staff there were dances, usually organised by Florence, and on special occasions a firework display, put on by Holthouse or Waring, provided the perfect end to evenings that became treasured memories.

Jesse's philanthropy led him to put money into a number of special projects in and around Nottingham, the city where he had been born and which always remained close to his heart. In 1908 he contributed substantial funds towards the rebuilding of the Albert Hall, Nottingham's leading Methodist centre, which had burned down in a disastrous fire. Jesse's contribution made it possible to erect a yet bigger and grander hall for the Methodist community and in addition he gave £5,000 for the construction of a new Binns organ and

Jesse and Florence at home with the children, John, Dorothy and Margery.

Plaisaunce, a large summer house, built by Jesse near Trent Bridge. Jesse loved to retreat to Plaisaunce, away from the everyday cares of work. He also invited staff to visit him there and he laid out tennis courts and a sports field around the house.

The Binns organ, at Nottingham's Albert Hall, built with the help of a substantial donation from Jesse.

Photograph taken at the laying of the foundation stone of the Dorothy Boot Homes in 1908. The Homes were built by Jesse for veterans of the Crimean War and Indian Mutiny. Some of the veterans are grouped together behind Jesse and Florence.

funded the organist's salary for a three year period. The money was donated on condition that popular organ recitals would be held at the hall on Saturday afternoons, with 'a fair number of seats at a charge of not exceeding 3d each', and that musical concerts arranged for Saturday evenings should be held 'for the purpose of promoting the love of high class music especially among the working classes'. Jesse was ever mindful of his humble origins. Also in 1908 he built the Dorothy Boot Homes, in Wilford, named after his eldest daughter, for veterans of the Crimean War and Indian Mutiny. A graceful curve of eleven almshouses, with a clubroom and library, looked out onto pleasant gardens, and regular social events were organised for residents and their families.

In recognition of his philanthropic works and his loyal support of the Liberal Party, Jesse was knighted in 1909. The ambitious young businessman from Nottingham's back streets had risen to be Sir Jesse Boot.

Boots Comrades in Khaki

This periodical is designed to maintain open lines of communication between headquarters and men from Boots serving with the colours, and to preserve and extend good fellowship among those who by faithful duty under Britain's banner and in the shops, offices, and warehouses, keep the old flag proudly flying.

Vol. I. APRIL Two
No. 1. 1915. Pence.

The gross receipts from sales will be contributed to a fund for the sick and wounded. See page 12.

SIR JESSE BOOT.

Boots
Chemists
STATION
STREET,
NOTTINGHAM.

Men from Boots,
 You who have hastened to serve actively in defence of King, of Country, and of Humanity, accept, please, a tribute of warm-hearted admiration and affection from us all at home.
 You are constantly in the thoughts of Lady Boot and myself. We know that you will acquit yourselves worthily, and we earnestly pray for your speedy and victorious return.
    Yours faithfully,

    Jesse Boot

Boots Birmingham branch. Its grand exterior, modelled on the company's Pelham Street store, in Nottingham, was calculated to impress the shopping public.

Boots fleet of Foden's steam vehicles.

THE DAWN OF THE twentieth century saw Jesse's business empire expanding in every direction. Branches of every size and description continued to open and each received the individual attention of Jesse and Florence. Particular pride was taken in the opening of prestigious shops in Princes Street, Edinburgh and on London's Regent Street. To ensure that every new branch and every new product was launched with maximum publicity, large adverts were placed in newspapers and trade journals and an unending torrent of handbills, posters and product catalogues rolled off the Island Street printing presses. To further encourage sales, Jesse offered counter assistants a handsome commission of five to ten shillings a week, provided the sales were of Boots own lines.

Jesse's empire became even more secure after the 1908 Pharmacy Act, which confirmed the legal right of large companies and stores, like Boots, to offer dispensing services. The decision settled a dispute that had dragged on for years between Jesse and many of his competitors, especially the private chemists.

Meanwhile a huge variety of pills, powders, pastilles, lozenges, tablets, creams, syrups, cough drops, toothpastes, soaps and perfumes continued to pour out of the Island Street and Parkinson Street factories. Many new products were developed at Boots own laboratories and other brands were rapidly acquired as Jesse took over company after company. To co-ordinate production and sales a team of 60 stocktakers travelled continuously up and down the country, visiting retail branches and sending back stock figures and details to Nottingham for checking and analysis.

An unexpected windfall for the company came with the passing of the National Health Insurance Act, in 1911, which extended medical benefits to ordinary working people. As a result there was a dramatic increase in the number of prescriptions issued by doctors, and as dispensing was restricted to qualified pharmacists, Boots dispensing branches found themselves busier than ever before.

Transport, as always, was vitally important to Boots and, ever eager to try out new ideas, Jesse purchased a Foden's 'box-type' steam vehicle that he had seen on display at the 1913 Agriculture Show at Colwick Park, Nottingham. Soon, a whole fleet of steam delivery vehicles was at work, huffing and puffing their way as far as Chesterfield, Burton-on-Trent, Sheffield, Birmingham, and even London.

Jesse was never content to simply let the business run itself. He was always looking at new ideas or fresh ways of improving the company and achieving further growth and progress. In 1913 Boots had a total of 560 branches scattered over England, Wales and Scotland and takings of more than £2.5 million a year.

But the real strength of Boots, the dedication of its staff and the commitment of Jesse himself, had yet to meet its greatest challenge - the outbreak of war. Following the assass-ination of Archduke Franz Ferdinand of Austria, in Sarajevo, on the 28 June 1914, the whole of Europe was plunged into a war that was fought on a scale never before imaginable.

In Nottingham there was constant talk of offensives and campaigns, and of loved ones far away. The Boot family was well aware of its responsibilities in these difficult times, and they all involved themselves in the war effort, in one way or another. John Campbell Boot, Jesse's eldest son, who had been in the cadet corps for six years and later joined the Territorials, was commissioned in the 7th Battalion Sherwood Foresters, serving with a transport unit in France. In the summer of 1914 John had married Joyce Pyman, the attractive daughter of a wealthy shipowner, and a year later they had the first of four daughters. Margery Boot, Jesse and Florence's youngest daughter, also went to France where she established a café and kitchen for wounded soldiers. On arriving in Northern France, Margery and her seven 'Lady Samaritans' were obliged to spend their first four months in a rickety wooden hut, before proper quarters could be found. To help raise funds for her daughter's pioneering venture, Florence organised a series of events in Nottingham. On the 24 July 1915 she put on a festival at Plaisance with choral entertainment, scenes from dramatic works and a programme of music by the Boots Plaisance band. In the afternoon, tea was served in a marquee and in the evening

Florence with her first grandchild.

there was 'dancing on the lawn to the strains of a string band'.

Boots was hard hit by the loss of staff abroad but the first thought of Jesse and Florence was for those men and women who had left their families to serve so many miles from home. To provide a link between Boots and company employees serving abroad Jesse started a newsletter, *Comrades in Khaki,* which included rolls of honour, obituaries, news about the company and letters from men at the Front.

In a patriotic editorial Jesse announced that the aim of the periodical was to 'extend good fellowship among those who by faithful duty under Britain's banner and in the shops, offices and warehouses, keep the old flag proudly flying'. Most telling of all in *Comrades in Khaki* were 'Letters from the Lads'. In April 1915 Private Farr, who had enlisted with the 7th Battalion Sherwood Foresters, from the Boots Shares Department wrote:

'Well, our change of life just now is not a happy one, I mean as regards the weather, (the rain) is simply pouring down in torrents, the trenches are 2 ft in water this morning, so we had to suspend operations'.

In December 1915 it was reported that a Boots pocket diary had been found on a man killed in the trenches who during the Christmas holiday had been in friendly contact with German soldiers entrenched only 200 yards away. In a short but sobering comment from the diary he had written: 'I went and exchanged greetings again and also exchanged cigarettes'.

A detachment of
Robin Hood Rifles
marching through
Nottingham on
the first stage of
their long journey
to France.

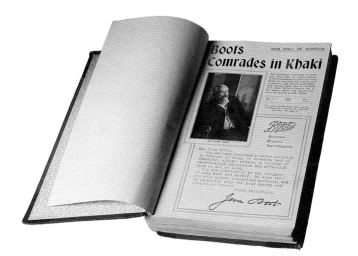

Front cover of
the first issue of
Comrades in Khaki.
Jesse set up the
newsletter to
provide a link
between the
company and its
employees at
the Front.

The laboratory at Island Street. The laboratory worked round the clock during the war to develop synthetic chemicals and pharmaceuticals needed both for the war effort and domestic needs.

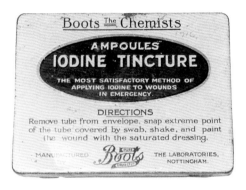

Iodine tin

As the war dragged on the country's demand for supplies and equipment became insatiable. In Nottingham, some of the city's larger firms were soon under pressure from the Government to consider ways in which they could contribute to the war effort. Jesse, even though he was worn out with overwork and the pain of his illness, responded with characteristic vigour. In a matter of months Boots was producing a remarkable variety of products, ranging from water sterilizers, vermin powder and anti-fly cream to pocket air pillows.

In July 1916 the praises of the Boots 'Iodine Ampoule', a tin of products for treating wounds and sores, were sung in a letter reproduced in *Comrades in Khaki,* though for rather an unexpected reason. In the course of action a Corporal Richardson, of the Chemical section of the Royal Engineers, had been hit by a bullet that had been deflected by the ampoule tin... 'This deflected the missile from his heart, which it missed by only an eighth of an inch. But for this he would undoubtedly have lost his life.'

To compensate for the loss of synthetic chemical imports from Germany, the Government looked to Boots for supplies of aspirin, disinfectant, saccharin, and other essential products. Jesse immediately began to enlarge the company's scientific laboratories and production facilities to put together a team of top class scientists to work on new products and recruited hundreds more female staff. A huge number of girls, at least 900, were employed in the manufacture of box respirators, used to help combat enemy gas attacks. The respirators were packed with granules that absorbed the gas. At one stage they were producing 90,000 respirators a week, giving a wartime total of more than 5 million.

Jesse also enlarged the company's transport fleet, and as most of the horses had been taken for military use he built up a fleet of steam vehicles and introduced several electrically operated vans. Whilst some industries, like Nottingham lace, had been dealt a near fatal blow by the First World War, the expansion of Boots industrial production ensured the company's survival.

The turmoil of war ended with the Armistice on the 11 November 1918. Peace had been won but at a terrible cost to families and nations throughout the world. After the war, Boots gradually re-stocked its shops with their full range of goods. In time new shops began to open again, new products appeared and new welfare schemes were introduced. In February 1920 the Boots Day Continuation School was opened on Station Street to develop part-time and day release courses for staff.

During the First World War the company introduced electrically operated trucks and vans to its transport fleet. They were ideal for short jouneys between the many Island Street warehouses.

Jesse, tired from years of work and the strain of the war years. At this time he began to think about selling the company.

John Boot relaxes in the sunshine.

But the stresses and strains of wartime had greatly worsened Jesse's arthritis and he was spending nearly every day in his wheelchair, barely able to move. He now longed to escape the long hours and drudgery of business. His old friend and loyal employee, Albert Thompson, had died in 1913, and an influx of new managers was struggling to introduce its own ideas into the company. It seemed to be the end of an era. Jesse finally had to admit that the company had become too much of a burden for him to carry. In this dejected mood he began to consider his company's future.

Most onlookers of the crisis assumed he would simply hand the company over to his son, John, but Jesse had other ideas. The relationship between Jesse and his son had always been cool and when, as a young man, John began to visit the theatre, attend concerts and go to late-night parties, Jesse concluded that John was nothing better than a rich playboy. On occasion John slipped away from work in the afternoon to attend late evening theatre showings in London, returning to Nottingham at six o'clock in the morning on the night mail train. In an attempt to put a stop to these jaunts, Jesse tried to insist that John was always present at the house every morning at eight o'clock to open the mail. Even after John returned from the war, much sobered and keen to settle down in the business, Jesse felt he could not trust his son with the company.

Hearing that Jesse might be willing to sell Boots to an outsider, Louis Liggett, the head of the United Drug Company, one of the largest pharmaceutical firms in America approached him with an offer to purchase the company for £2¹/₄ million, a price that was beyond Jesse's wildest dreams. Liggett was a loud-talking extrovert, a complete contrast to Jesse, yet, to his family's horror, Jesse invited Liggett to see him at St. Helier in the Park to discuss the proposal in more detail. With speculation and rumour running riot in the press, and amidst a storm of protest from John and Florence, the sale went ahead. The only concession made by Jesse to his son, in the sale agreement, was that John would be found an appropriate managerial position in the company.

John was devastated but ironically Liggett, unlike Jesse, recognised John's business talents and as soon as the sale had gone through he invited him over to America to widen his experience of company management and to consider ways in which Boots might be reorganised. Liggett also invited John Greenwood to America, a talented young Boots manager who was to become one of the company's most influential directors.

On examining Boots in some depth Liggett had discovered that Jesse had neglected some parts of his empire, and his reluctance to delegate had left many managers in a demoralised state. With John Boot's help, Liggett introduced a more modern system of management in Boots, which soon put the company back on its feet. And much to Jesse's surprise John Boot began to take on a leading role in the company's development. Within a few years Boots had recovered from its 1920 crisis and was once again able to look forward to the future with confidence.

The Times,
5 July 1920

Staff greet the Prince
of Wales, escorted
by John Boot, on his
visit to Island Street
in 1923.

The Prince of Wales
watches a tablet
machine in operation.

Excited staff gather
outside the Victoria
Station for a
memorable trip to the
British Exhibition at
Wembley on 24 June
1924. More than
5,000 staff visited
the exhibition and
travelled to Wembley
in a total of eight
special trains.

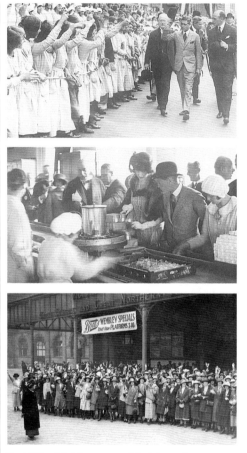

In 1923 a highly successful visit to the
Island Street works by the Prince of Wales,
hosted by John Boot and his fellow
directors, provided a further boost to
public confidence in the new-look Boots
company. The company's retail staff
magazine, the *Bee* ('Be Enthusiastic and
Efficient') reported that 4,000 staff
thronged Island Street to welcome the
Prince, swelled by hundreds more public
spectators. The magazine recorded that:

'The Prince took particular interest in an
automatic machine which was counting
and bottling Cascara Tablets working at the
rate of 20,000 tablets per hour, or, in other
words, packing 800 bottles in that time. He
enquired diligently into the various details,
and elicited the information that this
machine, which requires two girls to work
it, was doing three times the work that
could be done by hard labour. Other
details given him were that there were 600
girls employed in the Packed Goods
Department, turning out 50 million
packages a year, which included 150
different sorts of tablets, and 350 different
sizes of tablet packing'.

Another memorable highlight from the
Twenties was the staff outing to the British
Empire Exhibition at Wembley on the 24
June 1924. Such was the enthusiasm for this
event that Boots had to charter eight special
trains. A total of 5,500 production workers
descended on Wembley for the day, by far
the biggest single party that visited the
exhibition. A souvenir brochure issued to
employees described the delights of the
Australian, Canadian, African, Malaysian
and Indian pavilions and noted that displays
of Nottingham lace could be viewed in the
Palace of Industry, where there was also a
reconstructed Boots shop with an impressive
display of the company's products.

Jesse and Florence must have been very
heartened to see the company's continuing
emphasis on staff welfare. Employee
insurance and pension schemes had been
protected, and the *Bee* and *Beacon* were full
of news about staff interests in sports, music,
photography, needlework and outdoor
pursuits. Jesse must surely have been proud
that Boots, despite its takeover, had
remained true to his own aims and ideals.

A group of friends set
off for the Wembley
Exhibition.

A VISION
FOR THE
FUTURE

Zeppelin raid damage on Greyfriar Gate, September 1916.

'Sir Jesse Boot, later Lord Trent, wholly paralysed, and retired from the chairmanship of the great chain of chemists' shops he had founded, was given the Freedom of the City of which he had been such a benefactor. I watched Sir Jesse - wheeled in his chair into the Council Chamber in the Old Exchange Hall. He sat there, white-haired, patriarchal, while the Mayor called on the Town Clerk to read the illuminated scroll creating the new Freeman.'

From the autobiography of Cecil Roberts, *The Bright Twenties*.

Freedom of the City, Casket and Key, presented to Jesse by Nottingham Corporation in 1920.

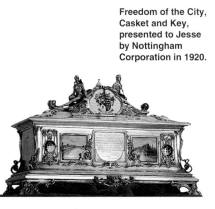

War Memorial Gates, the Victoria Embankment, built with the aid of funds from Jesse Boot. He also gave the land for the rest gardens.

AT THE END of the Great War people and nations all over the world began to look towards a new and better future. Caught up in this great tide of relief and hope, Jesse, despite his crippling arthritis, was determined to play a role in that future. Around him lay a city that had suffered a long battle against shortages, zeppelin attacks, grime and depression, but its spirit was undimmed. This was Jesse's Nottingham, his native city, in which he took undying pride.

Nottingham Corporation had lost no time getting war damage repaired, building new houses, tramways and roads, and initiating projects that would create employment. For Nottingham it was 'business as usual', an approach that Jesse could certainly respect. In this same spirit of recovery and renewal, Jesse gave £1,650 to a club for discharged soldiers and sailors and the handsome sum of £50,000 to Nottingham's General Hospital. And this was only the start. In the summer of 1920 he purchased 36 acres of open land that lay along the northern side of the Victoria Embankment alongside the River Trent right opposite his beloved Plaisaunce, for landscaping with a continuous sweep of parkland. The Embankment had been laid out with grass and trees so that in addition to forming a barrier against flooding, it created a pleasant walkway alongside the River Trent. The 'New Park' was an ideal complement to the Embankment, providing a large expanse of open land for public recreation and in the process providing ample playing fields for three schools in the Meadows area: Mundella Secondary, Collygate and Trent Bridge. As

Bank Holiday crowds stroll along the Trent Embankment, a part of Nottingham which held a special place in Jesse's affections.

part of the development an imposing war memorial gateway was built, with the aid of funds from Jesse Boot, along with a delightful rest garden.

In thanks for Jesse's benefactions 'for the welfare of his native city' he was presented with the honorary Freedom of the City of Nottingham on the 25 October 1920. Nothing could have pleased him more; and Jesse was soon discussing plans with Nottingham Corporation for yet another public park. In 1921 he helped Nottingham Corporation buy Woodthorpe Grange, a 40 acre estate that occupied an elevated position, to the east of the city. It made an invaluable 'open space' for Nottingham, a city which by the Twenties had grown to have a population of 275,000.

However Jesse had yet to reveal his greatest philanthropic scheme, the provision of an entire estate for new University College buildings for Nottingham. In November 1919 he had bought a large estate at Highfields, in Lenton, on the west side of Nottingham, with the intention of building a 'model' village along the lines of Cadbury's Bournville or Lever's Port Sunlight. With the sale of Boots, in 1920, Jesse was obliged to drop the village idea,

but only a year later his thoughts turned to an even more ambitious scheme for the Highfields Estate. For some time he had been discussing the possibility of establishing an East Midlands University with Edmund Huntsman, a Nottingham solicitor who had handled much of Jesse's legal work in the early 1900s. On one occasion after meeting with Huntsman in Jersey, Jesse sent Huntsman, the following day, a cheque for £50,000 to start a University endowment fund. At last the scheme was under way, though to become a reality the sponsors needed to find a large site to house the new University. However this problem was solved in the summer of 1921 when Jesse, who was visiting Nottingham, happened to be out with Huntsman on a drive through the Highfields Estate. On pausing to admire the view over the Trent valley, it was remarked that Highfields was an ideal site for a University campus. Jesse seized on the idea with all the enthusiasm of his youth and during the afternoon of the same day Jesse summoned Huntsman to his office to discuss the project. In fact the idea of building a University for the whole East Midlands was subsequently abandoned, though this proved to be very much to Nottingham's advantage.

'A few years ago the Clifton Estate offered for sale a piece of land on the Nottingham side of the Trent, almost facing Plaisaunce. We had often observed the great enjoyment of the large crowds frequenting the river banks on Saturday afternoons and Sundays, and I was keenly desirous that the river bank should be kept as open as possible. Therefore I purchased this land and presented it to the City of Nottingham to be preserved forever as an open space for the benefit of the citizens. Altogether I have the most pleasant recollections of the River Trent throughout my whole lifetime, and it has in fact become so endeared to me that it seems almost to be a living personality and an old friend.'

Jesse Boot, 1929

University College, Nottingham, before the new site was opened at Highfields. The College had been founded in 1881.

Work on Morley Horder's classical style Trent Building approaches completion. Horder had previously worked on the interior design of many of Jesse's shops. Jesse took a personal interest in every detail of the new building and its surrounding grounds.

For many years Nottingham had been desperately searching for a new site to replace its existing cramped University College buildings on Shakespeare Street near the City centre. Indeed no-one was more acutely aware of this than Huntsman, who was both on the City Council and the Council for University College. The College had been founded in 1881 and had grown rapidly, though its restricted site prevented any possibility of expansion. If the College was ever to achieve full University status it was essential to find a more appropriate site where new buildings could be constructed, with modern facilities and equipment.

It was a huge undertaking but Huntsman had the political influence to get the project started and Jesse had the money and the vision to see it through. Jesse's plan was to devote 35 acres of the site to the new University whilst the remainder would be landscaped into an extensive public park, with an ornamental lake, gardens, recreation grounds and a swimming bath, all to be set out below the valley crest which was to be crowned by the University's Trent Building. This was the very spot where Jesse and Huntsman had first conceived the idea for a new University site.

Jesse began to pour money into the scheme. £200,000 alone was spent on the building of a wide new road, University Boulevard, that would provide access to the south side of the University College and link Beeston with Lenton. Each side of the boulevard was flanked with grass verges, trees and ornamental shrubs. With the new road Jesse could then start work on the park layout and main buildings, engaging Morley Horder, who had worked on many of Boots stores, to execute a series of designs for the project.

Soon, the whole estate was being transformed. On the valley-top work began on the foundations for Horder's impressive Trent Building, that would come to dominate the new campus and park. The lake, laid out immediately below the Trent

University Boulevard, and the new University College only a few years after their completion. The whole site was originally part of Jesse's Highfields Estate, which he gave to University College in 1921. The College gained full University status in 1948.

Building, was created by enlarging the fishponds of Highfields House, a task which involved removing 350,000 tons of earth and gravel, some of which was used for making concrete foundations for the new University buildings. Horder constructed his Trent Building from Portland stone, adopting a classical style of architecture that lent the building a reserved dignity well suited to a new University while blending in perfectly with the surrounding landscape. As the new building rose on the horizon no one could be in any doubt that Nottingham's new University College was at last becoming a reality.

Now in his seventies Jesse found himself working as hard as ever. Because of his ever worsening state of health he spent an increasing amount of time in Jersey, which had many happy memories, for both Jesse and Florence, and which had the additional benefit of a mild climate that suited Jesse's arthritis. Eventually he bought a large house, Millbrook, at St. Helier which especially delighted Florence. She entertained local friends, politicians, artists and business people at a lively round of social events, so that Millbrook was always filled with life and laughter. Jesse enjoyed the social life at Millbrook but his thoughts were never far away from his projects back in Nottingham. One visitor to the house remembered that 'he was always busy, with a mass of secretaries coming in and out'. As his hands had become so painful he either dictated letters to one of his secretaries, sometimes just attempting a shaky signature, or, whenever possible, he used the telephone.

Jesse's signature, 1925. By this time his rheumatoid arthritis had made writing almost impossible.

Villa Millbrook, Jersey. Towards the end of his life Jesse spent much of the year in Jersey, where the warm climate suited his health.

Florence Boot, whose
lively personality
and artistic flair were
a constant source
of inspiration to
both Jesse and the
company. She died in
1952 aged 90.

During the winter he often travelled to the south of France, in search of warm weather, though such trips were never allowed to interrupt progress with his work. Few details regarding the Highfields project escaped his attention. Having received a set of plans for the University College sports pavilion from the registrar, he wrote back from his hotel in Cannes:

'I am not in favour of the flower borders against the Pavilion Walls; in the first place it is not a suitable place for flower beds, situated in the midst of high spirited young sportsmen, besides being unprotected from damage by cricket balls, footballs etc... the area would be more useful for cricketers awaiting their innings'.

He wrote frequent letters to the University registrar, Mr Shimeld, on every aspect of Highfields, urging him to obtain the best possible equipment for the science laboratories and even involving himself in the appointment of a groundsman for the sports grounds...'You will want a good man who understands tennis to look after all the tennis courts and bowling greens - the 24 hard courts will be in use all the year round and will consequently require constant attention'. Florence also took an active interest in the

project's development contributing, from her own money, funds for a women's hall of residence, Florence Boot Hall.

While Jesse spent day after day looking at estimates, designs and reports for the new University buildings and grounds, John Boot was just as preoccupied with a visionary project, started by Jesse in the early 1920s, to build a huge new manufacturing plant that would incorporate the very latest ideas of industrial production. Further expansion had become impossible at Island Street and Station Street where there was already a serious shortage of space, but John suggested a bold solution to the problem. This involved building a completely new industrial complex on land that Jesse had bought near Beeston, right opposite the Highfields Estate, originally with the intention of using it for his industrial village sheme. Inspired by John Boot's enthusiasm the directors appointed a works planning committee, early in 1927, to investigate the site's development potential. In under a year a major scheme had been approved for the construction of a large new soapworks on the site which was followed by vast new factory buildings for the manufacture, storage and distribution of 'Wet' and 'Dry' goods. John also had the foresight to buy up a large block of nearby land for the company's future development.

John was now working on a scale that his father must surely have admired. To design the new buildings he engaged the distinguished engineer Sir Owen Williams, who had designed the 1924 British Empire

Loading up at
Station Street. By
the late 1920s the
company was
desperately short of
space at Island Street,
Parkinson Street and
Station Street, and
John Boot began to
look for a completely
new production site.

Exhibition at Wembley, to create an industrial palace. As Jesse's University building neared completion at Highfields, a new era for Boots was dawning only a short distance away, in the Trent Valley, in the shape of an architectural triumph of concrete and glass. Sadly, Jesse did not live to see the opening of the 'Wets' building (D10), in 1933, but as the first pioneering buildings gradually rose out of the Trent Fields he knew his vision for the company's future was destined to become a reality. The same year saw the opening of the 1,000th Boots store at Galashiels in Scotland, another major landmark in the Company's progress towards the future.

Jesse did however live to see the completion of his Highfield's project. The new University College buildings were officially opened by King George V and Queen Mary on the 10 July 1928, on a day that marked the climax of Jesse's remarkable life. Nottingham's pride in its new University shone through the day's proceedings. The *Nottingham Journal* recorded that: 'The foundation of a University is a landmark in the history of any nation. The establishment in our own city of such a home of learning justifies all the jubilation which today will mark the occasion. For Sir Jesse Boot, the founder, it represents the climax of a great and meritorious career'.

From a background of struggle and poverty Jesse had built up a company that had become a household name all over Britain and then founded a new University in the City where he had been born and spent most of his life. Not long after the University's opening he was honoured with the title of 'Lord Trent of Nottingham'.

Boots pioneering 'Wets' factory (D10) at Beeston under construction. The engineer, Sir Owen Williams, used a dramatic combination of concrete and glass to create what has been described as 'a milestone in modern architecture'.

The 'Wets' factory, shortly after its completion, in 1933.

Opening ceremony of Nottingham University College, Highfields, on 10 July 1928. The ceremony was conducted by King George V and Queen Mary. Sadly, Jesse was unable to attend owing to his poor state of health. Its progress was however relayed to him in a nearby room and the King and Queen took tea with him afterwards.

Official opening of Nottingham's new Council House by the Prince of Wales on 22 May 1929. Huge crowds gathered to watch the ceremony. The Council House, with its council chamber, reception rooms and mayor's apartments, was designed by T Cecil Howitt. He started his career as a pupil with Albert Nelson Bromley, who was at that time working on Jesse's flagship store on Pelham Street in 1904.

Jesse's bust at the University's entrance gates. In front of him is the Boots Beeston site, with its factories, warehouses and office buildings. The inscription below the bust reads: 'Our great citizen Jesse Boot, Lord Trent. Before him lies a monument to his industry. Behind, an everlasting monument to his benevolence.'

The new University came at just the right time for Nottingham as, despite the problems of the Depression, the City Council had thrown itself wholeheartedly into a huge programme of public works during the 1920s. Major slum clearance projects were begun in the City itself, while in the suburbs large new housing estates were constructed, according to the latest town planning principles. In addition new health centres, schools, libraries, roads and tramways were built all over the city. And less than a year after the opening of the new University buildings, a grand new Council House, to replace the Old Exchange, was opened by the Prince of Wales. By the end of the decade Nottingham had become Queen of the Midlands and a city of national status.

For a year or two Jesse continued to follow the University's progress closely, and he kept a lively interest in Nottingham's activities, but his pain became unbearable and after a drawn-out struggle he died on the 13 June 1931, at the age of 81. At his memorial service, held at St Mary's church in Nottingham, his old friend Edmund Huntsman, who had become chairman of University College recalled that Jesse had never lost sight of 'a wonderful vision which stretched far into the future'. And that vision burned more brightly than ever in the hands of Jesse's son.

With all the energy and dedication of his father, John Boot threw himself heart and soul into developing the new site at Beeston, and in 1933, Boots was brought back into British control once again. With the support of an influential group of bankers John Boot approached Louis Liggett with an offer for the company. The offer was well timed as in America Liggett was struggling to cope with financial problems caused by the Great Depression. After four nerve racking months of bargaining, requiring all his persuasive powers, John Boot succeeded in regaining control of the company. To the delight of the family, the employees and the whole nation, Boots was once again back in British hands and Jesse's vision of the future was secure.

In the following years the Boots chain continued to expand; new products were developed and new welfare schemes were

John Boot, the second Lord Trent. Despite Jesse's reservations about his son, John proved a highly successful businessman. After winning back control of the company from Louis Liggett, he became Chairman and led Boots with all the energy and dedication of his father. At the time of his death, in 1956, Boots had become one of the country's leading companies.

introduced for staff. During the Second World War the company continued to manufacture a huge range of products to help the country's war effort. In the post-war years Boots products found world-wide markets and the company introduced a new generation of self-service shops to the High Street. Many of its products became established as household names. By the time of John's death in 1956, Boots had become one of the largest companies in Britain, with international interests and a turnover of millions.

Boots No7 range of cosmetics was introduced in 1935.

Today the Company occupies a unique place in the High Street of the United Kingdom and in the affection of its staff and customers around the world. Yet it all began with the dreams of a young boy called Jesse Boot who left school at the age of 13 to help his mother run a tiny herbal shop in Nottingham more than a hundred years ago.

Sources and further reading

The Boots Museum

Frank Barnes, *Priory Demesne to University Campus: a topographic history of Nottingham University,* University of Nottingham, 1993

Stanley Chapman, *Jesse Boot of Boots The Chemists: a study in business history,* Hodder and Stoughton, 1974

J E Greenwood, *A Cap for Boots: an Autobiography,* Hutchinson, 1977

R Iliffe & W Baguley, *Victorian Nottingham: a Story in Pictures,* Volume 18, Nottingham Historical Film Unit, 1977

Christopher Weir is a well-known local historian and author whose books include *Bygone Nottingham* and *The Nottinghamshire Heritage.*